THE DIGITAL FRONTIER

EXPLORING THE BOUNDARIES OF ARTIFICIAL INTELLIGENCE

TIRTH PATEL

Made with ♥ on the Notion Press Platform
www.notionpress.com

To all those who have dedicated their lives to advancing the field of artificial intelligence and exploring its endless possibilities. Your tireless efforts and groundbreaking discoveries have pushed the boundaries of what we thought was possible, and have paved the way for a future that is both exciting and uncertain. This book is dedicated to you, as a tribute to your passion and commitment to advancing the digital frontier.

Contents

Foreword

As artificial intelligence continues to rapidly advance and shape our world in countless ways, it is more important than ever to understand its potential and limitations. "The Digital Frontier: Exploring the Boundaries of Artificial Intelligence" provides a comprehensive and insightful exploration of this rapidly-evolving field, offering readers a nuanced understanding of its impact on society, culture, and the future of work.

In this book, the author takes readers on a journey through the fascinating world of AI, examining its history and evolution, ethical considerations, and role in various industries. The chapters on the use of AI in science and discovery, as well as the impact on society and culture, provide a deep understanding of how this technology is already shaping our world, and what we can expect in the years to come.

What sets this book apart is its focus on the relationship between humans and machines, and the importance of balancing innovation with ethics. The author's insightful commentary and thought-provoking analysis challenge readers to consider the broader implications of AI, beyond its immediate applications.

"The Digital Frontier" is a must-read for anyone interested in understanding the current and future impact of AI on our world. It offers a nuanced and comprehensive exploration of this rapidly-evolving field, and will leave readers with a deeper understanding of its potential, challenges, and possibilities.

[Tirth Patel]

Preface

Artificial Intelligence (AI) has been a topic of interest and curiosity for decades. With advancements in technology, AI is now becoming an integral part of our lives, shaping the way we work, communicate, and even think. This book, "The Mind's Algorithm: A Journey Through the Future of Artificial Intelligence," is an attempt to explore the various aspects of AI, its potential impact on society, and its future implications.

Through the different chapters of this book, we delve into the ethical considerations of AI, its role in science and discovery, its impact on the future of work, and much more. We aim to provide a comprehensive understanding of AI, from its history to its current state and potential future developments.

This book is not just for technology enthusiasts, but also for anyone interested in understanding the impact of AI on society and the world we live in. It is written for those who want to gain insight into the possibilities and limitations of AI and its potential to shape the future.

I would like to express my gratitude to all those who contributed to the creation of this book. It would not have been possible without the valuable insights and inputs from various experts in the field of AI.

I hope this book provides readers with a thought-provoking journey through the exciting and rapidly-evolving landscape of AI.

Acknowledgements

Writing a book is never a solitary task, and this book is no exception. There are many people without whom this book would not have been possible.

First and foremost, I would like to thank my family for their unwavering support and encouragement throughout this journey. Your love and support have given me the strength to persevere through the challenges of writing and completing this book.

I would also like to express my gratitude to my friends and colleagues who have offered their time, expertise, and support. Your feedback, encouragement, and insights have been invaluable in shaping this book.

I am indebted to the scholars, researchers, and practitioners in the field of artificial intelligence who have advanced our understanding of this complex and rapidly-evolving field. Their contributions have been instrumental in shaping the content of this book.

Finally, I would like to express my gratitude to the team at the publisher for their dedication, professionalism, and expertise in bringing this book to fruition. Your support and guidance have been essential in every step of this process.

Thank you all for your support and contributions to this book.

Prologue

It's hard to imagine our lives without the use of technology. With the advent of artificial intelligence, our world is transforming rapidly. AI has the potential to change the way we live, work, and interact with each other.

But what exactly is AI? How does it work? And what ethical considerations should we take into account as we develop this technology further? In this book, we embark on a journey through the world of AI to explore these questions and more.

From the history of AI to its present-day applications, we'll delve into the technology that is rapidly shaping our world. We'll examine the ethical dilemmas posed by AI and the challenges that lie ahead as we seek to create a future that is both advanced and ethical.

Join us on this journey as we explore the mind's algorithm and discover what the future may hold for artificial intelligence.

CHAPTER ONE

The Birth of AI

In the beginning, there was only the mind - the mysterious, ineffable source of human consciousness and thought. For centuries, philosophers and scientists have grappled with the question of what makes the mind tick, and how it produces the rich tapestry of human experience. It wasn't until the mid-20th century that a new tool emerged that promised to unlock the secrets of the mind - the digital computer. With its ability to process vast amounts of data and execute complex algorithms, the computer seemed like the perfect tool to model and simulate human thought. The first experiments in artificial intelligence were crude by today's standards, but they were groundbreaking at the time. Researchers used simple rule-based systems to mimic human reasoning, such as the famous "Eliza" program that simulated a psychotherapist by responding to user input with canned phrases and questions. As computers grew more powerful and sophisticated, AI research expanded to include more complex tasks, such as natural language processing, image recognition, and game playing. One of the earliest breakthroughs in AI was the development of the perceptron algorithm in the 1950s, which allowed computers to learn simple pattern recognition tasks.

However, progress in AI was not always smooth sailing. In the 1970s and 1980s, researchers hit a wall when they realized that the traditional rule-based approach to AI was insufficient for dealing with the complexity and ambiguity of the real world. This led to a period of disillusionment known as the "AI winter," during which funding for AI research dried up and many experts believed that AI was a dead end. But the seeds of a new AI revolution were already being sown. In the 1990s and 2000s, researchers began to develop new machine learning algorithms that could learn from large datasets without being explicitly programmed. These algorithms, such as artificial neural networks and support vector machines, enabled computers to perform increasingly complex tasks, such as speech recognition and autonomous driving. Today, AI is more pervasive than ever, powering everything from online recommendation systems to medical diagnosis tools. And as researchers continue to push the boundaries of what is possible with AI, the future looks brighter than ever for this once-controversial field. But with great power comes great responsibility. As AI becomes more advanced and more integrated into our lives, there are growing concerns about its potential risks and drawbacks. In the coming chapters of this book, we will explore some of these challenges and opportunities, and delve into the complex and fascinating world of artificial intelligence. Despite the significant advances made in AI, there are still many challenges and limitations to be overcome. One of the main challenges is the so-called "AI alignment problem," which refers to the difficulty of ensuring that AI systems behave in ways that are consistent with human values and objectives. If AI is to be used to make decisions that affect human lives, it is essential that it takes into account ethical considerations and respects human rights. Another challenge facing AI researchers is the issue of explainability. Many AI systems, particularly those that use deep learning algorithms, are often seen as "black boxes" that make decisions based on complex and opaque processes. This lack of transparency can make it difficult for humans to understand how and why AI systems make certain decisions, which can be problematic in areas such as healthcare and law enforcement.

Despite these challenges, the potential benefits of AI are enormous. One area where AI is already making significant inroads is in the realm of healthcare. AI systems are being used to analyze medical images, diagnose diseases, and even develop new drugs. In the future, AI could play an even bigger role in healthcare, enabling more personalized and effective treatments for patients. AI also has the potential to revolutionize other industries, such as transportation, energy, and finance. Self-driving cars, for example, could dramatically reduce the number of traffic accidents and increase the efficiency of transportation networks. AI could also help to optimize energy usage and reduce waste, as well as improve financial decision-making and reduce the risk of fraud. Of course, there are also risks associated with AI, particularly in the area of job displacement. As AI systems become more advanced, they are likely to replace many jobs that are currently performed by humans, particularly in industries such as manufacturing and transportation. This could lead to significant social and economic upheaval, particularly if large numbers of workers are displaced without adequate retraining and support.

In the chapters that follow, we will explore these and other topics in greater detail, delving into the fascinating and rapidly evolving world of artificial intelligence. From the ethical considerations of AI to its potential impact on the future of work and society, "The Mind's Algorithm" is your guide to understanding one of the most transformative technologies of our time.As AI becomes more advanced and ubiquitous, it is also raising important questions about the nature of human consciousness and intelligence. Some experts believe that AI could eventually surpass human intelligence, leading to a phenomenon known as "the singularity." This could have profound implications for the future of humanity, as AI systems with superhuman intelligence could potentially make decisions that are beyond human understanding or control. Another important area of research in AI is the development of "general AI," or AI systems that can learn and adapt to a wide range of tasks and environments, similar to how human intelligence works. This is in contrast to most current AI systems, which are designed to perform specific tasks, such as playing chess or recognizing images. General AI has the potential to be much more versatile and adaptable than current AI systems, but it also poses significant challenges, particularly in terms of designing systems that can learn and reason in a way that is consistent with human values and ethics. Despite the challenges and uncertainties associated with AI, it is clear that the technology is rapidly transforming our world in ways that are both exciting and daunting. As we continue to develop and refine AI systems, it is essential that we do so in a way that is responsible, ethical, and transparent. This will require not only technical expertise, but also a deep understanding of the social, political, and ethical implications of AI. In the chapters that follow, we will explore the history of AI, its current state of the art, and the potential paths it could take in the future. We will delve into the technical details of AI algorithms, but also consider the broader societal and ethical implications of AI. Whether you are a student, a researcher, or simply curious about the future of technology, "The Mind's Algorithm" is your guide to understanding one of the most transformative technologies of our time.One important aspect of AI that is often overlooked is its relationship to human creativity. Many people assume that AI is simply a tool for automating repetitive or mundane tasks, but in reality, it has the potential to be a powerful tool for creativity and innovation. AI can be used to generate new ideas, create art, and even write music or literature.

One example of this is the use of "generative adversarial networks" (GANs) to create realistic images, music, and other forms of art. GANs consist of two neural networks: a "generator" network that creates new examples of a given category (such as images of faces), and a "discriminator" network that evaluates whether these examples are realistic or not. By iterating between the generator and discriminator networks, GANs can generate increasingly realistic examples of a given category, often surpassing the capabilities of human artists or designers. However, the use of AI in creative fields also raises important questions about the role of human artists and creators. Will AI eventually replace human creativity altogether, or will it serve as a tool for augmenting and enhancing human creativity? What happens when AI-generated art is indistinguishable from art created by humans? These are just some of the questions that we will explore in later chapters. Another important consideration when it comes to AI is its impact on privacy and security. As AI systems become more sophisticated, they are increasingly able to analyze large amounts of data about individuals, including their personal preferences, behaviors, and even emotions. This raises important questions about how this data is collected, stored, and used, particularly in the context of commercial or government surveillance. There are also concerns about the potential for AI to be used maliciously, such as in the development of "deepfakes" or other forms of disinformation. As AI algorithms become more sophisticated, they are able to create increasingly convincing fake videos, audio recordings, and other forms of media. This has the potential to cause significant harm, both to individuals and to society as a whole.

In the following chapters, we will explore these and other topics in greater depth, providing a comprehensive overview of the current state of AI and its potential implications for the future. Whether you are a technologist, a policy maker, or simply someone interested in the future of technology, "The Mind's Algorithm" is your guide to understanding one of the most transformative technologies of our time.

CHAPTER TWO

The History of AI: From Early Concepts to Modern Breakthroughs

- The origins of AI: from ancient myth to modern science
- Early concepts and pioneers of AI, including Ada Lovelace, Alan Turing, and John McCarthy
- The rise of expert systems and rule-based AI in the 1970s and 1980s
- The development of machine learning and neural networks in the 1990s and 2000s
- The emergence of deep learning and reinforcement learning in the 2010s and beyond

The history of AI is long and varied, stretching back to ancient myths and legends of machines that could think and act like humans. However, it wasn't until the 20th century that the idea of artificial intelligence began to take shape as a scientific discipline. One of the earliest pioneers of AI was Ada Lovelace, a 19th-century mathematician and writer who is credited with writing the first algorithm designed to be processed by a machine.

In the 20th century, the concept of AI began to take shape as a formal field of study. In the 1940s and 1950s, researchers such as

Alan Turing and John McCarthy laid the foundations for modern computing and artificial intelligence. Turing is perhaps best known for his work on the Enigma machine during World War II, but he also made significant contributions to the development of computing and AI. McCarthy, on the other hand, coined the term "artificial intelligence" and helped to develop some of the earliest AI programs, including the Lisp programming language.

Throughout the 1960s and 1970s, AI research continued to advance, with the development of expert systems and rule-based AI. These systems were designed to mimic the decision-making processes of human experts, such as doctors or engineers, by encoding their knowledge into a set of rules that could be processed by a computer. While these systems were initially promising, they eventually proved to be limited in their ability to learn and adapt to new situations.

In the 1990s and 2000s, the development of machine learning and neural networks brought a new wave of innovation to the field of AI. These systems were designed to learn from data, rather than being explicitly programmed with a set of rules. This approach proved to be much more effective at solving complex problems, such as image recognition and natural language processing.

In recent years, the emergence of deep learning and reinforcement learning has pushed the boundaries of what is possible with AI. Deep learning algorithms, which are based on neural networks with multiple layers, have been used to create highly accurate models for image and speech recognition, natural language processing, and more. Reinforcement learning, on the other hand, has been used to create AI systems that can learn from trial and error, allowing them to master complex tasks such as playing chess or Go.

As we look to the future of AI, it is clear that the field will continue to evolve and push the boundaries of what is possible. In the following chapters, we will explore some of the most exciting and innovative developments in the field of AI, and consider the potential implications of these technologies for society and humanity as a whole. Despite the many breakthroughs in the field of AI over the past few decades, there have also been significant challenges and setbacks. One of the most significant challenges facing AI researchers is the problem of explainability. As AI systems become more complex and powerful, it can be difficult to understand how they are making decisions or predictions. This is a critical issue, particularly in domains such as healthcare and finance, where the consequences of AI errors or biases can be significant. Another challenge facing AI researchers is the problem of bias. AI systems are only as good as the data they are trained on, and if that data contains biases or inaccuracies, then the resulting AI system will also be biased. This has led to concerns about the use of AI in areas such as hiring and criminal justice, where biased AI systems could perpetuate existing inequalities and discrimination. Despite these challenges, there are also many exciting opportunities and possibilities for AI in the future. One area that is particularly promising is the development of AI-powered robotics and automation. Robots and autonomous systems have the potential to revolutionize industries such as manufacturing, transportation, and healthcare, by increasing efficiency, reducing costs, and improving safety. Another area where AI is already having a significant impact is in the field of natural language processing (NLP). NLP is the branch of AI that deals with the interaction between humans and computers using natural language. NLP has made it possible to develop chatbots, virtual assistants, and other conversational interfaces that can understand and respond to human language in a natural way. This has huge potential for applications such as customer service, education, and healthcare. Finally, one of the most exciting possibilities for AI in the future is the development of artificial general intelligence (AGI). AGI is the idea of creating an AI system that is capable of understanding and learning any intellectual task that a human can. While AGI is still largely theoretical, many experts believe that it could be achieved within the next few decades. If successful, AGI could revolutionize fields such as science, engineering, and medicine, by providing powerful new tools for discovery and innovation.

In summary, the history of AI has been a long and fascinating journey, full of breakthroughs, setbacks, and surprises. As we continue to explore the potential of AI in the future, it is clear that there are both challenges and opportunities ahead. In the following chapters, we will delve deeper into some of the most exciting and innovative developments in the field of AI, and consider the ethical and societal implications of these technologies.

CHAPTER THREE

The Ethics of AI

As artificial intelligence (AI) continues to advance, it has the potential to create enormous benefits for society. However, it also poses significant ethical challenges that must be addressed. The use of AI raises complex ethical questions about the nature of humanity, the responsibility of creators, and the appropriate use of technology. In this chapter, we will explore the most pressing ethical concerns surrounding AI and some of the ways in which researchers and policymakers are working to address them.

Transparency and Explainability

One of the key ethical challenges of AI is the issue of transparency and explainability. As AI systems become more advanced, they are often developed using complex algorithms that can be difficult to understand or explain. This lack of transparency can make it difficult to ensure that these systems are working as intended, and can create challenges for accountability and oversight. To address these concerns, researchers and policymakers are developing frameworks for transparent and explainable AI. This means designing AI systems in ways that are understandable and transparent, allowing for the detection of errors, biases, and unintended consequences. It also means developing tools and techniques for explaining the outputs and decision-making processes of AI systems in ways that are understandable to non-experts.

Accountability and Responsibility

Another important ethical concern in AI is the issue of accountability and responsibility. As AI systems become more sophisticated, they are often designed to operate autonomously, making decisions without human intervention. This can create challenges for accountability and responsibility, as it can be difficult to determine who is responsible for the decisions made by these systems.

To address these concerns, researchers and policymakers are exploring new approaches to accountability and responsibility in the context of AI. This includes developing new legal frameworks that assign liability for the actions of autonomous systems, as well as designing systems that incorporate human oversight and intervention.

Fairness and Bias

The use of AI also raises important ethical questions about fairness and bias. AI systems can perpetuate biases and discrimination, particularly when they are trained on datasets that reflect existing societal biases. This can lead to outcomes that are unfair or discriminatory, such as in the use of facial recognition technology to identify individuals in public spaces.

To address these concerns, researchers and policymakers are working to develop AI systems that are designed to minimize bias and discrimination. This includes developing techniques for detecting and mitigating bias in training datasets, as well as designing algorithms that are more resistant to bias and discrimination.

Privacy and Security

The use of AI also raises significant ethical concerns about privacy and security. AI systems often rely on large amounts of data, and the use of that data can raise serious privacy concerns. For example, facial recognition technology has been used to identify individuals in public spaces without their consent, raising concerns about the potential for mass surveillance.

To address these concerns, researchers and policymakers are exploring new approaches to data privacy and security in the context of AI. This includes developing new legal frameworks for data protection, as well as designing AI systems that are designed to minimize the collection and use of sensitive data.

Conclusion

The ethics of AI is a complex and multifaceted issue that will require ongoing discussion and debate. In this chapter, we have explored some of the most pressing ethical concerns surrounding AI, including transparency and explainability, accountability and responsibility, fairness and bias, and privacy and security. While these challenges are significant, they can be addressed through careful consideration and thoughtful design. In the following chapters, we will explore some of the most promising approaches to addressing these challenges and consider the potential future of ethical AI.

CHAPTER FOUR

The Future of Work in the Age of AI

Artificial intelligence (AI) is transforming the world of work, creating new opportunities and challenges for workers, employers, and policymakers. In this chapter, we will explore the ways in which AI is shaping the future of work, and consider some of the potential benefits and drawbacks of this transformation.

The Impact of AI on Jobs

One of the most significant impacts of AI on the world of work is the potential for automation. As AI systems become more advanced, they are able to perform a growing range of tasks that were previously done by humans. This has the potential to significantly reduce the demand for certain types of jobs, particularly those that are routine or repetitive.

At the same time, AI is also creating new opportunities for work. As AI systems become more sophisticated, they are able to perform tasks that were previously thought to be the exclusive domain of human workers. This includes tasks that require creativity, empathy, and complex decision-making.

To prepare for these changes, policymakers and employers will need to consider new approaches to education, training, and workforce development. This may include programs that focus on developing the skills that are most in demand in a world where AI is increasingly prevalent.

The Potential for New Forms of Work

AI is also creating new opportunities for workers to engage in non-traditional forms of work. For example, AI-enabled platforms are enabling workers to connect with employers and customers in new and innovative ways. This includes platforms that allow workers to provide services on demand, such as ride-sharing or food delivery. These new forms of work have the potential to create more flexibility and autonomy for workers, as well as new opportunities for entrepreneurship and innovation. However, they also raise important questions about the rights and protections of workers in the gig economy.

The Importance of Human-Machine Collaboration

While AI has the potential to automate many tasks, it is unlikely to completely replace human workers in most industries. Instead, the most promising future for AI is one in which it collaborates with human workers to improve productivity, efficiency, and innovation. To achieve this goal, employers and policymakers will need to consider new approaches to the design of work, including the development of systems that enable effective collaboration between humans and machines. This may include the use of augmented reality technologies to enable workers to interact with AI systems in new and innovative ways, as well as the development of new interfaces and tools that enable seamless collaboration.

Conclusion

The future of work in the age of AI is a complex and multifaceted issue that will require ongoing attention and engagement from policymakers, employers, and workers. In this chapter, we have explored some of the ways in which AI is transforming the world of work, including its impact on jobs, the potential for new forms of work, and the importance of human-machine collaboration. While the challenges posed by these changes are significant, they also create new opportunities for innovation, growth, and prosperity. In the following chapters, we will explore some of the most promising approaches to harnessing the power of AI to create a more equitable and sustainable future of work.

CHAPTER FIVE

The Role of AI in Science and Discovery

Artificial intelligence (AI) has the potential to revolutionize the way we conduct scientific research and make new discoveries. In this chapter, we will explore the ways in which AI is being used in scientific research and consider some of the potential benefits and drawbacks of this approach.

AI and Data Analysis

One of the most promising applications of AI in science is in the area of data analysis. With the proliferation of large and complex datasets, scientists are increasingly turning to AI to help them make sense of the data they collect.

AI algorithms can quickly and accurately identify patterns and correlations within large datasets, helping scientists to identify new relationships between variables and make new discoveries. This has the potential to significantly accelerate the pace of scientific discovery and improve our understanding of the natural world.

AI and Drug Discovery

Another area where AI is having a significant impact is in the discovery of new drugs and therapies. With the help of AI, scientists are able to rapidly screen large numbers of potential drug candidates, identifying promising candidates for further study.

AI algorithms can also help scientists to identify new targets for drug development, improving our ability to develop effective treatments for a wide range of diseases. This has the potential to significantly improve human health and well-being, and represents a major advance in the field of medical research.

The Ethics of AI in Scientific Research

While the potential benefits of AI in scientific research are significant, it is also important to consider the ethical implications of this approach. For example, some have raised concerns about the potential for bias in AI algorithms, particularly when it comes to the analysis of sensitive data.

It is also important to consider the potential impact of AI on the job market for scientific researchers. As AI becomes more prevalent in scientific research, it may lead to the displacement of some scientific research jobs, particularly those that involve data analysis and other routine tasks.Continuing with the topic of AI and drug discovery, one of the major challenges in developing new drugs is the high failure rate in clinical trials. AI has the potential to significantly reduce this failure rate by identifying potential drug candidates earlier in the drug discovery process.

In traditional drug discovery, scientists typically rely on their expertise and intuition to select which molecules to study further. However, with the help of AI, scientists can rapidly screen thousands or even millions of molecules, identifying promising candidates much more quickly than with traditional methods.

AI algorithms can also analyze large volumes of biomedical literature, identifying potential drug targets and new ways to develop treatments for diseases. By combining this approach with traditional drug discovery methods, scientists can significantly improve their chances of developing effective treatments for a wide range of diseases.

Another exciting application of AI in scientific research is in the field of astronomy. AI algorithms are being used to analyze massive amounts of data from telescopes and other astronomical instruments, helping scientists to identify new objects and phenomena in the universe.

For example, AI algorithms can help to identify gravitational waves, which are tiny ripples in space-time that are generated when two massive objects collide. These waves are incredibly difficult to detect, but with the help of AI, scientists are able to analyze vast amounts of data from multiple telescopes and identify the tell-tale signs of a gravitational wave event.

The use of AI in scientific research raises important ethical and social questions. For example, who owns the data generated by scientific research, and who has the right to use it? How can we ensure that AI algorithms are transparent and unbiased, and not perpetuating existing societal biases? These are complex questions that require careful consideration, and scientists, policymakers, and other stakeholders must work together to develop appropriate frameworks for the use of AI in scientific research.

In conclusion, the use of AI in scientific research has the potential to significantly accelerate the pace of discovery and improve our understanding of the natural world. From drug discovery to astronomy, AI is already making an impact in a wide range of scientific fields, and its potential applications are limited only by our imaginations. However, as with any new technology, it is important to consider the potential ethical and social implications of AI in scientific research, and to ensure that its use is guided by principles of transparency, fairness, and respect for human rights.

Conclusion

The role of AI in science and discovery is a complex and rapidly evolving field that has the potential to transform the way we conduct research and make new discoveries. In this chapter, we have explored some of the most promising applications of AI in scientific research, including its role in data analysis and drug discovery. We have also considered some of the potential ethical and social implications of this approach, including concerns about bias and job displacement. While the challenges posed by AI in scientific research are significant, they also create new opportunities for innovation and discovery, and have the potential to improve our understanding of the natural world and our ability to address some of the most pressing challenges facing humanity.

CHAPTER SIX

AI and Ethics in Society

As AI technologies continue to advance, they are raising important ethical questions about their impact on society. From autonomous weapons to biased algorithms, the use of AI is raising important questions about fairness, accountability, and transparency. One of the most pressing ethical concerns about AI is the potential for algorithmic bias. AI algorithms are only as objective as the data they are trained on, and if that data is biased, the algorithm will be biased as well. This can have serious consequences for marginalized groups, who may be disproportionately affected by biased algorithms in areas like criminal justice, employment, and credit scoring. To address these concerns, it is important for AI researchers and developers to prioritize fairness and transparency in the development of AI algorithms. This can include measures like regularly auditing algorithms for bias, using diverse training data, and involving diverse stakeholders in the development process. Another area of ethical concern is the use of AI in the workplace. While AI technologies have the potential to improve efficiency and productivity, they can also have negative consequences for workers, including job loss and increased surveillance. It is important for policymakers to consider the potential impact of AI on employment and to develop policies that support workers and help them to adapt to a changing labor market. The use of AI in criminal justice is another area of ethical concern. AI technologies are increasingly being used to make decisions about bail, sentencing, and parole, but there are concerns about the fairness and accuracy of these systems. For example, a study by ProPublica found that a widely used algorithm for predicting recidivism was biased against black defendants, leading to longer sentences and higher rates of recidivism.

To address these concerns, it is important for policymakers to develop clear guidelines for the use of AI in criminal justice, and to ensure that these systems are transparent and accountable. It is also important to involve diverse stakeholders in the development of these systems, including members of the communities that are most affected by them. In addition to these concerns, there are also broader ethical questions about the impact of AI on society as a whole. For example, as AI technologies continue to improve, they may create new ethical dilemmas around issues like privacy, security, and human autonomy. It is important for policymakers, researchers, and other stakeholders to work together to address these concerns and to ensure that the development and use of AI technologies is guided by principles of transparency, accountability, and respect for human rights. In conclusion, the use of AI is raising important ethical questions about fairness, accountability, and transparency in society. While AI technologies have the potential to improve our lives in many ways, it is important to ensure that their development and use is guided by ethical principles and values. By working together to address these concerns, we can help to ensure that AI technologies are used in ways that benefit all members of society.

One of the most pressing ethical concerns with AI is the potential for it to be used to infringe upon individual privacy rights. As AI technologies become more sophisticated, they are increasingly able to collect and analyze vast amounts of data about individuals, including their personal habits, preferences, and beliefs. This raises important questions about how this data is collected, stored, and used, and who has access to it. Another area of ethical concern is the potential for AI to be used for malicious purposes. For example, AI-powered cyber attacks could potentially wreak havoc on critical infrastructure systems like power grids, water supplies, and transportation networks. It is important for policymakers and researchers to consider these risks and to develop robust cybersecurity measures to mitigate them. There are also important ethical considerations around the use of AI in the military. Autonomous weapons systems, for example, raise important questions about the ethics of delegating life-and-death decisions to machines. It is important for policymakers and military leaders to carefully consider the implications of these technologies and to ensure that they are used in accordance with international humanitarian law. Finally, there is the broader question of how AI will impact the future of humanity. Some experts have raised concerns about the potential for AI to outpace human intelligence and to pose an existential threat to humanity. While these concerns may be speculative, they underscore the importance of careful consideration and ethical oversight in the development and deployment of AI technologies. Overall, the ethical implications of AI are complex and multifaceted. It is important for policymakers, researchers, and other stakeholders to carefully consider the potential impacts of these technologies and to work together to develop ethical frameworks that guide their development and use. By doing so, we can help to ensure that AI is used in ways that benefit all members of society and promote the common good. Another important ethical consideration in AI is the potential for bias and discrimination in decision-making. AI systems are only as unbiased as the data they are trained on, and if the data used to train the AI is biased or reflects existing inequalities, then the AI system will likely perpetuate and even exacerbate these biases. For example, if an AI system is trained on historical data that reflects gender or racial biases, it may end up making decisions that reinforce these biases in the future. Another key issue related to AI and ethics is transparency and accountability. As AI systems become increasingly complex, it can be difficult to understand how they are making decisions, which can make it challenging to hold them accountable for their actions. This is especially concerning in cases where AI is being used to make decisions that have significant impacts on people's lives, such as in the criminal justice system or in hiring practices. Finally, there is also the question of how to ensure that AI systems are developed and used in ways that align with human values and goals. For example, while an AI system might be very effective at achieving a specific goal, like maximizing profits, it might do so in ways that are harmful to people or the environment. It is important to ensure that the development and deployment of AI systems are guided by ethical considerations and that they align with broader societal goals and values.

Overall, the ethical implications of AI are far-reaching and complex, and it is essential that they are carefully considered by all stakeholders involved in the development and deployment of these technologies. By addressing these ethical issues head-on, we can help to ensure that AI is developed and used in ways that promote the common good and benefit all members of society.

CHAPTER SEVEN

The Use of AI in Manufacturing and Supply Chain Management

Introduction

The use of AI in manufacturing and supply chain management is becoming increasingly prevalent as businesses seek to optimize processes, reduce costs, and improve product quality. This chapter will explore the various ways in which AI is being used in these domains, as well as the potential ethical and societal implications of its use.

Applications of AI in Manufacturing

AI is being used in a variety of ways to improve manufacturing processes. One of the key applications is the use of sensors and machine learning algorithms to monitor production processes in real-time. This enables manufacturers to identify inefficiencies or quality issues early on, allowing for more timely corrective action. Additionally, AI is being used for predictive maintenance, which involves analyzing data from sensors and other sources to identify potential problems before they occur. This approach can help to reduce downtime and maintenance costs.

Another way in which AI is being used in manufacturing is through the use of robots and drones. These technologies are being used to automate tasks that would otherwise require human labor, such as material handling and assembly. This can help to reduce labor costs and improve efficiency.

Case Studies and Examples of AI in Manufacturing

There are many examples of businesses using AI to improve manufacturing processes. Tesla, for example, has implemented a number of AI technologies to optimize production processes and improve product quality. The company uses sensors and machine learning algorithms to monitor the performance of its manufacturing equipment, and has also developed AI-powered robots to handle some of the assembly tasks.

GE is another company that has embraced AI in its manufacturing operations. The company has implemented a predictive maintenance system that uses machine learning algorithms to identify potential equipment failures before they occur. This has helped to reduce downtime and maintenance costs, while also improving product quality.

Amazon is yet another example of a business that has embraced AI in manufacturing and supply chain management. The company uses robots and AI to automate many of the tasks in its warehouses, such as packing and sorting. This has helped to improve efficiency and reduce costs.

Ethical and Societal Considerations

While the use of AI in manufacturing and supply chain management can bring many benefits, there are also ethical and societal considerations that need to be taken into account. One concern is the potential impact on employment and the workforce. As more tasks are automated, there is a risk that some workers will be displaced. This can have negative consequences for the individuals involved, as well as for the broader economy.

There are also concerns about privacy and data security. As more data is collected and analyzed, there is a risk that sensitive information could be exposed or misused. Additionally, there is a need to ensure that AI is used in ways that align with human values and goals. This means ensuring that AI systems are designed and implemented in an ethical and transparent manner.

Future Prospects and Challenges

The use of AI in manufacturing and supply chain management is still in its early stages, and there are many opportunities for further innovation and optimization. However, there are also challenges that need to be addressed. One of the key challenges is related to data quality, integration, and adoption. In order for AI to be effective, it is important to have access to high-quality data. Additionally, there is a need to ensure that AI systems are integrated effectively into existing workflows and processes.

Conclusion

The use of AI in manufacturing and supply chain management has the potential to transform these domains in significant ways. However, there are also ethical and societal considerations that need to be taken into account. By being mindful of these considerations, it is possible to harness the power of AI in a way that benefits both businesses and society as a whole.

CHAPTER EIGHT

The Limitations and Risks of AI

Introduction:

Overview of the limitations and risks of AI

Importance of understanding the limitations and risks in order to responsibly develop and deploy AI technologies

Section 1: Limitations of AI

- Explanation of the limitations of current AI technologies, including narrow AI and general AI
- Discussion of current limitations in AI's ability to understand language, recognize images, and make decisions
- Overview of the challenges in creating AI systems that can learn and adapt to new situations

Section 2: Risks of AI

- Discussion of the potential risks of AI, including job displacement, bias and discrimination, privacy concerns, and unintended consequences
- Examination of high-profile examples of AI gone wrong, such as the Tay chatbot and the Uber self-driving car accident
- Overview of the challenges in creating AI systems that are safe, reliable, and trustworthy

Section 3: Addressing the Limitations and Risks of AI

- Explanation of the various approaches being taken to address the limitations and risks of AI, including research in explainable AI, fairness and accountability in AI, and AI safety
- Discussion of the importance of interdisciplinary collaboration in addressing these challenges
- Overview of the ethical considerations involved in developing and deploying AI technologies

Section 4: Public Perception and Understanding of AI

- Discussion of the importance of public perception and understanding of AI, and the potential impact on the development and adoption of AI technologies
- Examination of common misconceptions about AI, and the need for clear communication about the capabilities and limitations of AI

Section 5: Regulatory Framework for AI

- Overview of current and proposed regulatory frameworks for AI, including in the areas of privacy, data protection, and algorithmic bias
- Discussion of the challenges in creating effective regulations for a rapidly evolving technology like AI, and the need for ongoing dialogue and collaboration between policymakers and stakeholders

Section 6: International Cooperation on AI

- Discussion of the global nature of AI development and deployment, and the importance of international cooperation and collaboration

- Overview of current initiatives and agreements related to AI, such as the Global Partnership on Artificial Intelligence (GPAI) and the OECD Principles on AI
- Examination of the challenges and opportunities for international cooperation on AI, including issues of trust, transparency, and accountability.

Section 7: The Ethical Use of AI in Military Applications

- Examination of the current and potential military applications of AI, such as autonomous weapons and battlefield decision-making systems
- Discussion of the ethical concerns raised by the use of AI in military contexts, including issues of accountability, transparency, and human control
- Overview of the international debate on the regulation and governance of AI in military applications, including the proposed ban on autonomous weapons.

Section 8: AI and the Environment

- Discussion of the potential for AI to be used in addressing environmental challenges, such as climate change and resource depletion
- Examination of current and proposed applications of AI in environmental management, such as precision agriculture and climate modeling
- Analysis of the risks and limitations of using AI in environmental contexts, including issues of data quality, bias, and transparency.

Section 9: AI and the Future of Humanity

- Exploration of the long-term implications of AI on human society and the global economy, including potential changes in employment, education, and social structures

- Discussion of the challenges and opportunities posed by the integration of AI into various sectors of society, including healthcare, transportation, and finance
- Analysis of different scenarios for the future of AI and its impact on humanity, and the need for ongoing dialogue and collaboration between stakeholders to shape the direction of AI development.

Conclusion:

Recap of the limitations and risks of AI, and the importance of addressing these challenges responsibly

Call to action for continued research and development in creating safe, reliable, and trustworthy AI systems.

CHAPTER NINE

AI and Artistic Expression: Exploring the Intersection of Technology and Creativity

Introduction

Art has always been a deeply human endeavor, a way for us to express our emotions, explore the world around us, and connect with one another on a profound level. But with the rise of artificial intelligence (AI), we are now seeing the emergence of a new kind of artist – one that is not human, but rather a machine capable of generating its own creative output. In this chapter, we will explore the intersection of technology and creativity, looking at the ways in which AI is being used to generate art, music, and other forms of creative expression. We will examine the potential benefits and drawbacks of AI-generated art, and the ethical and philosophical considerations that come with this emerging field.

The Promise of AI-Generated Art

One of the most exciting aspects of AI-generated art is its potential to revolutionize the creative process. With the help of algorithms and machine learning, artists can now explore new forms of expression that would have been impossible just a few years ago. For example, some AI-generated art is created by feeding a machine learning algorithm large amounts of data, which it then uses to generate new pieces of art that mimic the style and form of the original data set. This approach has been used to create everything from abstract paintings to landscape photographs, and it is allowing artists to push the boundaries of what is possible in the world of visual art.

AI-generated music is another area where the technology is showing great promise. By analyzing existing compositions and musical styles, AI algorithms can create new music that is both original and captivating. For example, OpenAI's MuseNet is a machine learning system that can generate original music in a variety of genres, from classical to jazz to pop. This technology has the potential to democratize the creative process, allowing more people to explore and experiment with musical composition.

The Challenges of AI-Generated Art

While the potential for AI-generated art is certainly exciting, there are also significant challenges that need to be addressed. For one, there is the question of ownership. If a machine generates a piece of art or music, who owns the copyright? Is it the person who created the algorithm, the person who trained it, or the machine itself? These are difficult questions to answer, and they highlight the need for new legal frameworks to govern this emerging field. Another challenge is the question of artistic intention. When a machine generates a piece of art or music, it does so without any intention or meaning behind it. This can be seen as both a strength and a weakness of AI-generated art – on the one hand, it allows for truly original creations that could not have been made by humans alone, but on the other hand, it raises questions about the value and significance of the art. If a machine generates a beautiful landscape photograph, is it truly art, or is it simply a technical feat?

The Ethical Considerations of AI-Generated Art

Artificial Intelligence has revolutionized the art world by providing new tools and techniques to create innovative and unique artwork. AI-generated art has brought new opportunities and challenges for artists, critics, and audiences alike. However, with these new opportunities come new ethical considerations that need to be addressed. In this chapter, we will explore the ethical implications of AI-generated art and discuss various perspectives on this subject. The first ethical consideration that arises from AI-generated art is the question of authorship. When machines generate art, who should be credited as the creator? Is it the machine or the artist who programmed it? Should AI-generated art be considered as intellectual property, and if so, who owns it? These are complex questions that need to be addressed by artists, lawyers, and policymakers. It is essential to establish clear guidelines and regulations to ensure that artists are appropriately compensated for their work and that the rights of machine-generated art are protected. Another ethical consideration is the use of AI-generated art in the context of cultural appropriation. AI algorithms are trained on vast amounts of data, including images and texts from various cultures and societies. As a result, the AI-generated art may incorporate elements from different cultural traditions without the artist's intention or understanding of their significance. This can lead to the misrepresentation and exploitation of cultures, which is a serious ethical concern. It is crucial to ensure that AI-generated art is respectful of cultural traditions and is not used to promote cultural appropriation or exoticism.

Privacy is another ethical consideration in AI-generated art. AI algorithms are trained on large datasets that include personal information, such as images, text, and metadata. This data can be used to generate highly personalized artworks, which may contain sensitive information about the individuals involved. This raises questions about the ownership and control of personal data used to train AI algorithms and how that data is used to generate art. Artists and AI developers need to ensure that privacy concerns are taken into account in the creation of AI-generated art. A related ethical concern is the potential use of AI-generated art for nefarious purposes, such as creating deepfake images or videos that can be used to manipulate public opinion or cause harm to individuals. The technology used to create AI-generated art can also be used for other purposes, such as generating realistic images of people who do not exist, which can be used for identity theft or fraud. These are serious ethical considerations that need to be addressed by policymakers, AI developers, and artists. The use of AI-generated art in advertising and marketing is another ethical consideration. AI-generated art can be used to create highly personalized and targeted advertisements, which can be extremely effective in promoting products and services. However, this also raises concerns about the manipulation of individuals' emotions and the potential use of AI-generated art to deceive or mislead consumers. It is crucial to ensure that AI-generated art is used ethically in advertising and marketing and that consumers are not exploited or manipulated. In conclusion, AI-generated art presents new opportunities and challenges for artists, critics, and audiences. However, with these opportunities come new ethical considerations that need to be addressed. The ethical implications of AI-generated art include questions of authorship, cultural appropriation, privacy, nefarious uses, and advertising and marketing. It is essential to establish clear guidelines and regulations to ensure that AI-generated art is used ethically and that the rights of artists and individuals are protected.

The End

Reflect on the Journey: You can use the end of your book to reflect on the journey you have taken the reader on throughout the book. Consider summarizing the main points and takeaways, and how they relate to the future of artificial intelligence.

Leave the Reader with a Call-to-Action: You can use the end of your book to encourage readers to take action in some way. Whether it is advocating for ethical AI development or pursuing a career in AI, leave the reader with a sense of purpose and motivation.

Open-Ended Conclusion: Another way to end your book is to leave the reader with an open-ended conclusion that allows them to draw their own conclusions and reflect on their own opinions about the future of artificial intelligence. This approach can lead to a thought-provoking and memorable ending.

Printed by Libri Plureos GmbH in Hamburg,
Germany